AS Sport & Physical Education
UNIT 2

AQA

Module 2: Sociocultural & Historical
Effects on Participation in Physical Activity
& their Influence on Performance

Symond Burrows

Philip Allan Updates
Market Place
Deddington
Oxfordshire
OX15 0SE

tel: 01869 338652
fax: 01869 337590
e-mail: sales@philipallan.co.uk
www.philipallan.co.uk

This Guide has been written specifically to support students preparing for the AQA AS Sport and Physical Education Unit 2 examination. The content has been neither approved nor endorsed by AQA and remains the sole responsibility of the author.

Printed by MPG Books, Bodmin

Environmental information
The paper on which this title is printed is sourced from managed, sustainable forests.

Contents

Introduction

■ ■ ■

Content Guidance

■ ■ ■

Questions and Answers

Introduction

About this guide

This guide is written to help you prepare for the Unit 2 test, which examines the content of **Module 2: Sociocultural and Historical Effects on Participation in Physical Activity and their Influence on Performance**. There are three sections to this guide:

- **Introduction** — this provides advice on how to use the unit guide, an explanation of the skills required by Module 2 and suggestions for effective revision.
- **Content Guidance** — this summarises the specification content of Module 2.
- **Questions and Answers** — this provides examples of questions from various topic areas, together with answers to these questions and examiner's comments on how they could have been improved. It concludes with a mock unit test. A mark scheme is provided with guidelines to enable you to assess your answers and identify your strengths and weaknesses.

An effective way to use this guide is to read through this introduction at the beginning of your course to familiarise yourself with the skills required for AS Sport and Physical Education. Try to make a habit of following the study skills and revision advice offered in this section. It may also help to refer back to this information at regular intervals during your course.

The Content Guidance section will be useful when revising a particular topic because it highlights the key points of each subsection of the Module 2 specification. You may want to tick off topic areas as you learn them to make sure that you have revised everything thoroughly.

The Question and Answer section will provide useful practice when preparing for the unit test. This practice should increase your awareness of exam-technique issues and maximise your chances of success.

Finally, you should attempt the mock unit test and use the mark scheme to assess your answers.

The specification

In order to make a good start to Module 2, it is important to have a close look at the specification. If you do not have a copy of this, either ask your teacher for one or download it from the AQA website — **www.aqa.org.uk**.

The specification describes the content of the modules and gives information about the unit tests. It is important for you to understand the following key terms used in the specification:

- **analysis** — a detailed examination to find the meaning or essential features of a topic
- **characteristic** — a feature or key distinguishing quality
- **definition** — a clear, concise statement of the meaning of a word
- **function** — the purpose of a specific role
- **initiative** — a new action taken to cause change
- **strategy** — a plan to achieve a particular goal
- **transition** — change or passage from one stage to another

In addition to looking at the specification, it would be useful for you to read the examiners' reports and mark schemes from previous Unit 2 tests (these are available from AQA). These documents show you the depth of knowledge that examiners are looking for, as well as pointing out common mistakes and providing advice on how to achieve good grades. Previous papers are very useful for practice. However, when taking the unit test, you should not simply repeat answers from a previous exam mark scheme. Questions may appear to be the same, but sometimes they are not! Read each question very carefully and answer the tasks as they are set.

Study skills and revision strategies

All students need good study skills to be successful. This section provides advice and guidance on how to study AS Sport and Physical Education, together with some strategies for effective revision.

Organising your notes

PE students can accumulate a large quantity of notes and it is useful to keep this information in an organised manner. The presentation is important: good notes should always be clear and concise. You could try organising your notes under main headings and subheadings, with key points highlighted using capitals, italics or colour. Numbered lists are useful, as can be the presentation of information in the form of tables or simple diagrams, for example:

It is a good idea to file your notes in specification order, using a consistent series of headings, as illustrated below:

> **Module 2: The nature and characteristics of physical activities**
>
> *PE: aims and objectives*
> These include:
> - development of physical skills
> - development of social skills
> - development of mental skills

At a convenient time after lessons, it is worth checking your understanding of your notes. If anything is still unclear, ask a friend to explain, do some further reading or ask your teacher for help.

Organising your time

It is a good idea to make a revision timetable to ensure you use your time effectively. This should allow enough time to cover *all* the relevant material. However, it must also be realistic. For many students, revising for longer than an hour at a time becomes counterproductive, so allow time for short relaxation breaks or exercise to refresh the body and mind.

Improving your memory

There are several ways to improve the effectiveness of your memory. Organising the material will help, especially if you use topic headings, numbered lists and diagrams. Reviewing and condensing your notes will also be useful, as will discussing topics with teachers and other students. Using mnemonics (memory aids) can make a big difference. For example, a mnemonic for the key characteristics of sport is:

- **S**erious
- **P**rowess involved
- **O**fficials present
- **R**ule governed/strict rules structures/national governing bodies
- **T**ime phased/strict time constraints

Revision strategies

To revise a topic effectively, you should work carefully through your notes, using a copy of the specification to make sure everything is covered. Summarise your notes to the key points using the tips given on note making above. Topic cue cards, with a summary of key facts and visual representations of the material, can be useful. These are easily carried around for quick revision. Finally, use the Content Guidance and Question and Answer sections in this book, discussing any problems or difficulties you have with your teachers or other students.

introduction

In many ways, you should prepare for a unit test like an athlete prepares for a major event, such as the Olympic Games. An athlete trains every day for weeks or months before the event, practising the required skills in order to achieve the best result on the day. So it is with exam preparation: everything you do should contribute to your chances of success in the unit test.

The following points summarise some of the strategies that you may wish to use to make sure your revision is as effective as possible:

- Use a revision timetable.
- Ideally, spend time revising in a quiet room, sitting upright at a desk or table, with no distractions.
- Test yourself regularly to assess the effectiveness of your revision. Ask yourself: 'Which techniques work best?' 'What are the gaps in my knowledge?' Remember to revise what you *don't* know.
- Practise past paper questions to highlight gaps in your knowledge and understanding and to improve your technique. You will also become more familiar with the terminology used in exam questions.
- Spend time doing 'active revision', such as:
  - discussing topics with fellow students or teachers
  - summarising your notes
  - compiling revision cue cards
  - answering previous test questions and self-checking against mark schemes
  - watching *Sky Sports News* or *Transworld Sport* to increase your knowledge of relevant up-to-date sporting examples of contemporary issues (e.g. drugs controversies, national governing body initiatives and foul play in sport).

Revision progress

You might find it useful to keep track of how your revision is going by drawing up a table similar to the one below, including topics in the first column.

Module topic: development of PE in state elementary schools	Revised (N/P/F)	Self-evaluation (1–5)
• Elementary school drill at the end of the nineteenth century		
• Model course of physical training		
• 1919 child-centred syllabus		
• 1933 PT syllabus		
• Developments in state PE in the 1950s		
• National Curriculum PE		

Complete column 2 to show how far you have progressed with your revision:

N = Not revised yet

P = Partly revised

F = Fully revised

Complete column 3 to show how confident you are with the topic:
5 = high degree of confidence
1 = minimal confidence — the practice questions were poorly answered

The table should be updated as your revision progresses.

The unit test

Unit Test 2 involves choosing three from four structured questions. Mark allocations vary, but are generally 3–5 marks. It is important to spend some time reading the questions in their entirety to make sure you can attempt all parts of the question, rather than just the first part, which is often the easiest.

There are 57 marks available in this test, which lasts for 1 hour and 15 minutes (giving you just over 1 minute per mark). The questions are short and may use pictures or diagrams as stimulus materials. If reference to the stimulus material is asked for in the question, you *must* refer to it in your answer.

Lines are provided on which to write your answers and additional blank pages are available at the back of the question–answer booklet. You should avoid squashing your answer into the available space because this can make it difficult to read. Do not write answers in the left- or right-hand margin because these are for the examiner's use.

Questions may have some words emphasised. This is to draw your attention to key words or phrases that you need to consider in order to answer the question. Sometimes, questions require structured headings to help you organise your responses. Make sure you write the appropriate answer under the correct subheading.

There are a number of terms commonly used in unit tests. It is important that you understand the meaning of each of these terms and that you answer the question appropriately.

- **Compare** — point out similarities and differences.
- **Define** — give a statement outlining what is meant by a particular term.
- **Describe** — provide an accurate account of the main points in relation to the task set.
- **Discuss** — describe and evaluate, putting forward the various opinions on a topic.
- **Explain** — give reasons to justify your answer.
- **Identify** — show understanding of unique or key characteristics.
- **State/give/list/name** — give a concise, factual answer.
- **What?/why?/where?/who?/how?** — these indicate direct questions requiring concise answers.

Whatever the question style, you must read the wording very carefully, underline or highlight key terms or phrases, think about your response and allocate time according to the number of marks available. Further advice and guidance on answering Unit 2 questions is provided in the Question and Answer section of this book.

The day of the unit test

On the day of the test, make sure that you have:

- two or more blue/black pens
- a watch to check the time
- water in a clear bottle to keep you hydrated (Unit 2 follows Unit 1, so you are likely to be in the exam room for over 3 hours!)

Make sure that you allow plenty of time to arrive, so that you are relaxed.

Read each question very carefully so that your answers are appropriate and relevant. Make sure that your writing is legible (you will not be awarded marks if the examiner cannot read what you have written). If you need more room for your answer, look for space at the bottom of the page or use the spare sheets at the end of the booklet. If you do this, alert the examiner by adding 'continued below', or 'continued on page X'.

Time is sometimes a problem. Make sure you know how long you have for the whole test. If you finish early, check your answers, adding more points to ensure you gain as many marks as possible. This is your one chance to impress the examiner — so take it!

Content
Guidance

Module 2 can be divided into three main topic areas:

- The nature and characteristics of physical activities
- Historical developments in sport and physical education
- Historical and social influences on modern-day sport

You may already be familiar with some of the information in these topic areas. However, it is important that you know and understand this information exactly as described in the specification. This summary of the specification content highlights key points. You should therefore find it useful when revising for the Unit 2 test.

In addition to summarising the specification content, this section includes examiner's tips, while at the end of some sections is a list of points entitled 'What the examiner will expect you to be able to do'.

Remember that this Content Guidance section is designed to support your revision and must be used in conjunction with your own notes.

The nature and characteristics of physical activities

Towards a concept of play

Key features of play include:
- fun and enjoyment
- spontaneity
- simple or childlike behaviour
- flexible, self-agreed rules (n.b. not 'no rules')
- flexible, self-agreed time–space boundaries

The main function of play for a child is to master reality (i.e. what it is to take on an 'acceptable role' in society). Through play, *children* learn many things, including:
- physical skills, such as coordination
- social skills, such as making friends
- cognitive skills, such as decision making
- moral skills, such as fair play
- emotional skills, such as accepting defeat
- environmental skills, such as safety awareness

The key functions of play for an *adult* include escaping from reality. Play provides stress relief, relaxation and recuperation from daily duties.

Physical and outdoor education

PE can be defined as 'a formally planned and taught curriculum, designed to increase knowledge and values through physical activity and experience'.

Aims of National Curriculum PE

Knowledge/values derived from PE	Examples
Physical and motor skills	Coordination; body awareness
Health and fitness	Physical activity in lessons; knowledge of the body; benefits of exercise
Preparation for active leisure	Encouragement and education about the benefits of continuing physical activity into adulthood
Personal value of self-realisation	Achieving success; increasing self-confidence and self-esteem
Socialisation and social skills	Making friends; improving communication skills
Leadership	Opportunities to lead or captain a group or team

PE has National Curriculum status as a compulsory subject from 5–16 years of age because it has a number of important functions in relation to pupils gaining such knowledge and values.

These aims and objectives, listed overleaf, can be achieved via the set PE curriculum. In addition, schools offer extra-curricular options for:

- sporting involvement (e.g. playing competitively for the school netball team)
- recreational involvement (e.g. open-access badminton club)

These provide further opportunities for the development of the national curriculum aims.

Teaching National Curriculum PE

National Curriculum PE:

- has been developed to provide equal opportunities for all pupils
- is compulsory for all children aged 5–16 — it is one of the foundation subjects
- focuses on a number of skills, including:
  - physical activity and a healthy lifestyle
  - safety practices
  - use of ICT within PE

Provision should be made for pupils with special educational needs, while programmes of study have been set for various age groups with attainment targets for each.

As one of the last foundation subjects to be put into practice, PE has faced strong competition for curriculum time. In 1994 there was a review of National Curriculum PE and a number of changes were made, including:

- a greater emphasis on games
- greater flexibility and choice at Key Stage 4 (an attempt to address the problem of the 'post-school gap')
- opportunities for schools to increase time for PE

PE content of the Key Stages

- **Key Stage 1** — gym, dance and games are compulsory.
- **Key Stages 1 and 2** — basic individual skills are developed, both individually and in small-sided games.
- **Key Stages 3 and 4** — a wider range of activities is offered.

At Key Stage 4:

- there are opportunities to specialise in particular activities
- there is development of more complex skills in competitive situations
- there are opportunities to experience a variety of roles, such as **performer**, **coach** and **official**

PE as an examination subject

PE became an examination subject because of various pressures, including:

- attempts to raise the status of the subject by an all-graduate profession

- the need for accountability, bringing PE in line with other 'more academic' subjects as exam results are analysed and published
- the need to provide better preparation for higher education or a career in PE or sport

Outdoor and adventurous education

Outdoor and adventurous education (OAE) is a compulsory part of PE. It can be defined as 'the achievement of educational objectives via guided and direct experience in the **natural environment**'. Examples include mountain walking and climbing. The purposes and functions of OAE are summarised in the diagram below.

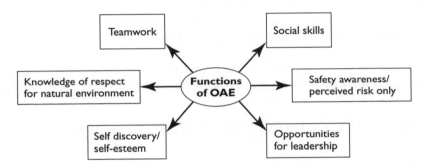

Despite its compulsory status as part of National Curriculum PE, OAE in most schools tends to be of relatively low quality, for example orienteering around the school grounds. There are a number of reasons for this, including:

- cost
- lack of qualified or motivated staff
- lack of time in a lesson
- parents and/or teachers deterred by the inherent risks

Leisure

Leisure time is **free time**. People have the opportunity to *choose* what to do. It is a time to refresh and renew their strength after toil. Leisure is time without obligation.

Some theories suggest that leisure is:

- a **spare-time** activity. Leisure helps restore people's energy for work. Practical leisure activities are viewed as non-serious; inactivity is due to laziness. (This stems from the protestant work ethic, i.e. work is Godly; leisure is lazy.)
- a **class-orientated** activity, related to position in society. The 'leisured class' has a right to leisure; the working classes must work hard to win the right to it. This concept is linked to traditional beliefs and to exclusivity.
- a **social process** activity. Leisure can help in social control; it should be available to everyone; friendships can be formed through leisure activities.

- a **creative fulfilment** activity. Leisure assists in moral and social development. It allows people to relax and enjoy themselves. It helps them become aware of their limits and to prove themselves.

The reasons for increased leisure time in modern-day society include the following:
- Mechanisation of labour has led to less time at work for many.
- Labour-saving devices in the home have created more free time.
- Societal expectations have led to demands for more free time in which to relax in an increasingly stressful society.

Preparation for leisure in schools

- Key stage 4 in particular allows each student to experience different roles, such as a **performer** in a variety of activities, a **coach** and a **referee**.
- Links are developed with local leisure centres and sports clubs.
- Teachers provide enjoyable curricular and extra-curricular PE experiences to encourage life-long participation (i.e. active leisure).

Physical and outdoor recreation

Recreation can be defined as the 'active aspect of leisure'. It is entered into **voluntarily** during free time and individuals have a **choice** about which activities to take part in. Recreation is similar to play in its relatively unsophisticated nature, limited organisation and emphasis on taking part as opposed to winning. People take part in recreational activities to relax, to relieve stress and to improve their health and fitness. Opportunities arise to meet people and socialise in a relatively informal environment.

Outdoor recreation

Outdoor recreational activities take place in the natural environment. This gives people the opportunity to experience at first hand the aesthetic beauty of the countryside and to learn to respect and appreciate the natural environment.

For some individuals, outdoor recreation provides a sense of adventure. The adrenaline buzz from situations involving **real risk** (e.g. skiing off piste during the time of an avalanche warning) is what makes recreation in the outdoors appealing to them, in addition to the other benefits.

Individuals may experience **perceived risk**. This means a feeling of danger when the situation is safe, for example when abseiling down the side of a rock face while wearing a safety harness and under the control of qualified instructors.

Subjective danger refers to the potential for individuals' own mistakes (e.g. slipping while abseiling with an instructor), but allows beginners to work in controlled, simple environments, i.e. where the risk is perceived. **Objective danger** is for more experienced participants who want to work in more complex surroundings where the elements are less predictable and more dangerous, i.e. there is a real risk.

Sport

Sport is defined by a number of key features. It involves **competitiveness** (i.e. the will to win) and is **serious**, particularly at the top, elite level. **National governing bodies** (e.g. the Football Association) look after the interests of, and try to develop the popularity of, a particular sport. They also provide strict **rule structures** that are enforced in **competitions** by **officials**. Sport requires high levels of physical **skill** (prowess) and **effort** (endeavour) in order to succeed and gain the **extrinsic rewards**, such as trophies or money, that are on offer.

The levels of seriousness, commitment and skill in sporting involvement vary. Some individuals are talented enough to take part professionally (i.e. for a living). Others participate in sport as amateurs during their leisure time.

Sport is, therefore, different from recreation in that it is competitive, strict rules apply and extrinsic rewards are available.

Tip The more of these characteristics you can identify, the more likely it is that an activity can be classified as sport.

The characteristics of sport and physical recreation are compared in more detail in the table below.

Sport	Physical recreation
Less immediate pleasure than in recreation; pain may be involved	Immediate pleasure
There may be extrinsic rewards	Participation provides intrinsic rewards and enjoyment
Time constraints on training or length of game	Length of participation is the individual's own choice
Serious training required	Level of training is the individual's own choice
High fitness and skill levels demanded, particularly as a professional	High levels of fitness and skill are not necessarily required

When participating in sport, performers adopt various **codes of behaviour**, which can be viewed on a continuum:

Sportsmanship   **Gamesmanship**

- Treat opponents with respect
- Fair play
- Play within the rules or etiquette of the activity

Example: kick the ball out of play if an opponent is injured — improves the atmosphere of the game

- Lack of respect for opponents
- Use of unfair practices to gain an advantage
- Often against etiquette of activity

Example: playing on, despite an obvious injury to an opponent — could lead to ill-feeling

Sports/PE classifications

National Curriculum PE

The National Curriculum divides PE into six categories:

- athletic activities
- outdoor and adventurous activities
- swimming
- gymnastics
- games
- dance

The AQA specification breaks up this classification and introduces three sub-categories of competitive sport.

Athletic sports

- Performance is measured quantitatively. The winner is the athlete who, for example, runs fastest, jumps highest, throws the furthest or lifts the heaviest weight.
- There is little tactical demand as performers use well-practised techniques and have relatively few technical movements to perfect. Tactics that are employed include reading the weather, deciding whether to compete in each round of a field event and pacing in races.
- There is no direct opposition. Athletes either take turns to perform or run in lanes, with no direct contact allowed.

Game sports

- The winner is the team or individual that achieves territorial domination and scores, for example, more points, goals or runs against the opposition.
- Players compete directly against opponents who are deliberately interactive and interfere with play.
- Players continually have to read the game and make decisions. The tactical demand is high.
- Players are dependent on **open skills** because games occur in a continually changing environment and require a high level of decision making.

Gymnastic sports

- The winner is the gymnast whose movements are judged to be the best in qualitative terms, measured against a pre-determined set of criteria.
- Gymnasts usually perform alone; opposing competitors place no direct interference on other gymnasts and are non-interactive.
- Competitors have little decision-making at the time of performance because most decisions have been made beforehand in the design of the routine.
- Gymnasts have to master a large number of techniques. Execution of a gymnastic routine requires great precision and consistency.
- Gymnastics consists of **closed skills** because the environment is fixed and there is little decision-making involved.

Pre-planning in gymnastic activities and team games

Gymnastic activities

- Gymnasts take it in turns to perform. Opponents cannot interfere directly with each other, which means the opposition does not need to be studied beforehand.
- Gymnastic sequences are choreographed (worked out) beforehand, i.e. they are pre-planned.
- Gymnasts need a back-up plan in case errors are made during a performance.

Team games

- Team-game performers are in direct opposition to their opponents, who attempt to interfere with their performance.
- Team-game performers have to make many instant decisions because their performance cannot be systematically pre-planned.
- Games players do use pre-planned ideas such as set plays, game plans and an overall approach to the game, but these may have to be adjusted as the contest develops and according to the opposition.

Interaction in game, gymnastic and athletic sports

Interaction refers to decisions based on the behaviour of team-mates and opponents.

- The territorial domination aspect of games promotes interaction.
- Gymnastic sports do not generally promote interaction because there is no direct interference from opponents and competitors take it in turns to perform. However, there might be some limited interaction, such as encouragement and advice from team-mates.
- Athletic sports do not promote much direct interaction in most events because direct interference is not allowed; competitors are often in lanes or take it in turns to perform. However, there can be indirect interaction with opponents in athletic sports, such as tactical decisions to do with pacing.

The performance pyramid

A pyramid structure can be used to illustrate a continuum of development from mass participation at its base through to excellence at the top.

Sporting
elite

Sport
for all

Excellence
Elite performers/highly skilled/fully
committed to gaining success

Performance
Skilled performers/regularly
train/perform to try and improve

Participation
Recreational involvement (e.g. for
fun/social/health and fitness benefits)

Foundation
Grassroots/basic introduction
to sport (e.g. at primary school)

What the examiners will expect you to be able to do

There is always a range of questions from the nature and characteristics of physical activities section of the specification. They could require:

- listing or identifying key features or characteristics of a concept (e.g. play, leisure, recreation or sport)
- key values/purposes of PE/OAE
- a comparison between different concepts (e.g. sport with recreation)
- the application of a variety of different concepts to a specified activity (e.g. swimming as play, sport, PE or recreation)
- classification and analysis of sports, often by comparing the scoring systems and tactical demands of athletic, gymnastic and game sports

Tip Apply your knowledge of concepts to the question as appropriate and you won't go too far wrong.

Historical developments in sport and PE

The influence of sports history on current-day provision of PE and sport in Britain can be studied in a number of stages:

- **popular pre-industrial recreation** (sports and pastimes, for example mob football)
- how sport played a part in **public school developments** in the **nineteenth century**
- the **rationalisation of sport** in an urban industrialised society
- the **development of state PE**

Popular pre-industrial recreation

Popular pre-industrial recreation covers activities and pastimes undertaken by most of the population before the rationalisation and development of sports. Mob football is an example of such an activity.

Key features of mob football and their social determinants are given in the following table.

Feature	Social determinant
Limited structure with few rules	Illiterate peasant population
Cruel and violent	Harsh society
Local versions	Limited travel and communications
Played infrequently on festivals or holy days	Limited free time

The influence of public schools on sport in the nineteenth century

English public schools in the early nineteenth century were characterised by a number of features:

- **controlled by trustees** — endowed status
- **exclusivity** — elitist, fee-paying schools for the gentry
- **rural locations** — boarding was necessary
- **single sex** — boys only
- **strict discipline** — flogging was common

The characteristics identified above were commonplace in public schools in the first part of the nineteenth century, before the Clarendon Commission Report. The 'big nine' public schools were investigated by the Earl of Clarendon in 1864. His report contained criticisms of many aspects of public-school life and gave advice on how schools could improve.

Sport was a **key reforming influence** in public schools such as Rugby and Eton. A major influence on such reforms was Dr Thomas Arnold, the liberal headmaster of Rugby School. Arnold's aim was to establish **social control**, with boys behaving better without the need for severe punishments imposed by masters. He wanted to establish a more trusting relationship between masters and **sixth formers**. In return for acting as role models and Arnold's 'police force' around school, the sixth formers were given increased status and powers of discipline. The main aim of such reforms was to produce **Christian gentlemen** with **high levels of morality**. Almost as a by-product, the status, regularity and organisation of games also increased.

As public schools such as Rugby continued to expand, the **house system** also grew. Individual houses (where the boys lived) became the focus of boys' social, recreational and sporting existence. Inter-house games kept boys out of trouble during the day and used up excess energy.

The increased playing of games required more organisation. Rules and regulations were written to govern how an activity should be played. Sixth-form boys performed a key role in ensuring that games were played to such rules in a more disciplined and controlled manner than previously. Team games became high priority in public schools as the **cult of athleticism** led to an obsession with the values of playing team games such as rugby football.

Athleticism

Athleticism combined **physical effort** with **moral integrity** (i.e. playing hard with sportsmanship). The main values of athleticism can be remembered as follows:

- **A**ll-round, mind and body
- **T**emperament
- **H**ealth
- **L**eadership
- **E**ndeavour
- **T**eamwork
- **I**ntegrity
- **C**ohesion and competition
- **I**nstrument of education
- **S**portsmanship
- **M**uscular Christianity

Muscular Christianity was concerned with the ethical values of sports participation. The ideas of **teamwork** and **loyalty** to the cause were seen as key qualities developed through sporting pursuits. Muscular Christianity combined **godliness** with **manliness** and sports performances were dedicated to God. Fair play and rule keeping in sport were of key importance.

The spread of athleticism

Athleticism spread via:

- the old boys network
- universities — national governing bodies and codification
- army officers — into forces
- clerics — into church groups, such as the YMCA
- sons of industrialists — to workers
- teachers — into other schools
- improved communications

Team games

Team games and leadership

Team games were used in public schools to help prepare boys to become leaders in society. The rationale behind this included that:

- being a captain in sport is preparation for leadership roles in society
- leadership requires strength, courage and bravery
- team games developed decision-making qualities
- organisational experience was gained

Team games and social control

Games acted as a form of social control in the following ways:

- The introduction of rules acted as a behavioural or etiquette code for the players.
- Teams were selected on ability.
- Older boys were helped during practice by younger boys.
- Schoolmasters gained the respect of pupils by supporting and participating in some games (e.g. cricket).

Development of rationalised sport in an urban industrialised society

The mid-nineteenth century onwards was a key time in the development of many sports. Ex-public schoolboys were highly influential in such developments in a number of ways:

- Games were taken to universities.
- They were involved in organised sport in public schools or returned to schools as coaches and spread the 'gospel' of athleticism.
- They were prominent in forming the national governing bodies of sport, clubs, leagues and rules.
- Athleticism was spread to parishes by curates and old boys working for the church.
- Athleticism was spread to the troops and the colonies by old boys serving as military officers.

As indicated above, ex-public schoolboys were highly influential in the formation of the national governing bodies of sport. They realised the need for rules and codification to ensure that sports were played in a more regulated manner.

In the second half of the nineteenth century, more fixtures were being played and more leisure clubs were being formed. These required rules, leagues and competitions. There was a clear need for such leagues to be well coordinated.

The development of **professionalism** and **subsequent commercialism** in sport in the late-nineteenth century had to be controlled because the middle and upper classes wanted to maintain control of sport and preserve their **amateur ideals**.

Development of mob games into a rational form

There were a number of social factors that influenced the development of mob games into a rational form, including:

- lack of space in an urban environment
- need for entertainment of the masses (e.g. association football as a spectator sport)
- transport developments (e.g. railways)

- more leisure time for the working classes (e.g. Saturday half-day)
- more disposable income for the working classes to spend watching sport
- middle- and upper-class desire for a civilised, disciplined workforce

Characteristics of rational recreation

The characteristics of rational recreation in an urban industrialised society included:
- played regularly to set rules as a result of more free time and improved literacy levels
- ethos of fair play and respectability as a result of the influence of public schools and the middle class
- elements of both amateurism and professionalism, reflecting the class structure
- played in purpose-built facilities as technology advanced
- played regionally, nationally and internationally as transport improved

Tip Some characteristics of rational recreation can be remembered using the letter 'r':
- respectable
- regular
- rule-based
- refined

Sport and the working classes

The emergence of sport for the working classes was hard won. Initially, migration to towns was met with gloom and poverty for many and there was a resultant lack of interest in sport. Indeed, the working classes were effectively excluded from most sports until the twentieth century because of factors such as lack of time, money and physical resources. The rules and codes of membership of many sports were designed by the upper classes to exclude the working classes. The exception to this was association football.

Development of PE in state elementary schools

Physical activity in state elementary schools progressed from **military drill** to **physical training** and then to **physical education**. Each stage involved changes in:
- **content** (e.g. lesson activities/subject matter)
- **objectives** (e.g. aims of lessons)
- **methods** (i.e. teaching styles used to deliver the lesson)

Wars such as the Boer War and the First and Second World Wars were key influences on these changes. For example, the poor performance by Britain in the Boer War led to the 1902 Model Course of Physical Training, which included the development of fitness and discipline as key aims.

Military drill, physical training and physical education each had distinct content, objectives and teaching methodology that reflected society's view of children at particular times during the twentieth century. At the start of the twentieth century, these were very much linked to obedience, discipline and fitness. As the century progressed, fitness remained important. However, as a result of changing views and teaching methods, there was more self-expression and decision-making by children.

From drill to physical education

Elementary school drill at the end of the nineteenth century

The 1870 Education Act made the setting up of board schools (state elementary schools) possible. Attendance for 5–10 year olds was compulsory. Space for play and physical exercise was restricted and specialist PE equipment was in short supply.

Drill was taught to youngsters by non-commissioned army officers (NCOs), to improve fitness and discipline. The style of delivery was **authoritarian**.

Different types of drill (e.g. military (1870) and Swedish (1890s)) were delivered by NCOs, and eventually by qualified class teachers, to develop obedience and discipline in working-class children. Familiarity with weapons was also developed in boys as preparation for military roles.

The Model Course of Physical Training (1902)

This was a time when military needs became more important than educational theory. Military drill was delivered in a command style to boys and girls of all ages by army NCOs. Physical training was dull and repetitive, but cheap, allowing large numbers to be instructed in small spaces. The Model Course came about as a result of the poor performance by Britain in the Boer War (1899–1902). The main aims of the Model Course were to develop obedience and discipline and to prepare children, particularly boys, for military service.

Early physical training (PT) syllabuses

The first of these was produced in 1904. The Model Course was revised and a compromise was established between military drill and the more therapeutic Swedish version of drill. There was more emphasis on exercise in the open air for its health-giving effects. Changes in fashion led to less restrictive clothes, allowing freer movement in lessons, which were now increasingly delivered by trained teachers.

The 1909 syllabus still aimed to develop obedience and discipline, but also covered more therapeutic effects of PT through exercises that involved work on posture, breathing and circulation. Teaching methods still included command delivery to children in ranks or in unison, but also allowed teachers some freedom of choice, enabling more enjoyment of physical activity.

The 1919 child-centred syllabus

The 1919 syllabus was progressive. It had a much broader content and was the first syllabus with a **child-centred approach**. It was set against the background of huge loss of life in the First World War. In addition, women had taken on 'men's work' during the war and proved their ability to cope physically with the demands this placed upon them. Women experienced raised social status and began to demand more equality in society, including in education.

The syllabus of 1919 emphasised **enjoyment** and **play** for under-7s, with **therapeutic** work the main aim for the over-7s, thus showing some differentiation between ages. More free movement, dance and 'small-game' playing were included in lessons, allowing teachers greater choice in both *what* to deliver as well as *how* to deliver.

The 1933 PT syllabus

The 1933 syllabus **differentiated** clearly between ages (i.e. one section for under-11s; another section for over-11s). Lessons still had an emphasis on physical skills and good posture. The key aim for teachers was development of both the mind and the body. The 1933 syllabus had a more varied content, with athletics, gymnastics and games skills included. Delivery was mainly by a direct style with some group work. Also, in solving problems as individuals, children were allowed to learn more at their own pace.

The 1933 PT syllabus was a watershed between the syllabus developments of the past and the physical education of the future, with its more varied aims, content and teaching methodology.

Developments in state PE in the 1950s

The Second World War emphasised the need for '**thinking soldiers**', which led to a drive for '**thinking children**'. Physical activities and facilities for children in schools were expanding and there was a far more open approach to PE. This is in evidence in the books *Moving and Growing* (1952) and *Planning the Programme* (1954), which were designed to help teachers deliver the curriculum more effectively. Problem-solving tasks were introduced that could be solved in different ways. Modern educational dance methods influenced the 'creative movement' approach, which was becoming more prominent at the time.

The Education Reform Act (1988)

This Act led to the introduction of National Curriculum PE, which applies to all state schools. The status of PE was reinforced by being made compulsory for all 5–16 year olds. National Curriculum PE aims to ensure that all children have similar experiences, irrespective of where they live in the country. However, there are differences in the time allowed and the facilities and equipment provided.

A comparison of drill with PE in the 1950s

Questions set in relation to the development of state PE often require a comparison to be made. Military drill and PE in the 1950s, when *Moving and Growing* was a key syllabus development, are compared in the table below.

Military drill	PE in the 1950s
No apparatus	Use of apparatus
Limited space	More space available
No choice of activity	Individual choice allowed
Individual exercise	Group situations
Regimented exercise	Play and freedom of movement
Marching and regimented exercise	Skills and minor games rather than exercise
No change of clothing	Specialist clothing

Issue analysis: sport in schools

You have to be able to review and show your understanding of current initiatives and strategies in school sport.

Development of sport in children

Awareness of the **TOPSport** scheme at primary level and the existence of **specialist sports colleges** in the secondary sector is required.

Various national agencies support the development of sporting activity in school children. The **Youth Sports Trust**, for example, has played a key role in providing **progressive pathways** through which children can develop. TOPS and Dragon Sport (Wales) programmes have also played a key role in this, particularly in relation to providing child-friendly equipment and resources for a variety of different sporting activities. Primary school teachers can use these in conjunction with resource cards detailing quality ways of delivering practical sessions. To develop further confidence in delivering TOPS programmes, teachers and sports leaders are given quality training.

Sports colleges

Central government policies on school PE and sport have seen a number of initiatives put in place designed both to increase the numbers taking part and to raise standards of performance. Secondary schools can apply for specialist status in a variety of areas, including sport. A **sports college** is a secondary school that has been granted specialist status for sport. Financial benefits are gained from this, so sports colleges can afford excellent facilities and top-level coaching. More curricular and extra-curricular time for PE is often provided. In order to support talented individuals in particular sports, sports colleges form links with national governing bodies and the United Kingdom Sports Institute (UKSI) network (e.g. tennis at Burleigh Community College in Loughborough with its local institute of sport at Loughborough University).

Sports colleges are also required to develop positive links with primary schools, special schools and the local community to provide opportunities for all to become active.

School Sport Coordinators programme

School Sport Coordinators are often based at sports colleges. They work to try to improve the quality and quantity of after-school sport and inter-school competition across their designated 'families' of schools. One way of doing this is to provide PE and sport courses for the ongoing professional development of teachers and other adults.

Provision for sport

Organisations involved in sport and recreation can be divided into three different groups:

- **Public-sector** organisations are **owned by local authorities** and trade on a profit-and-loss basis. Key aims for these public-sector organisations are high-quality recreational services and the promotion of mass participation in sport.
- **Private-sector** organisations are **privately owned businesses** that promote activities to make a **profit**. In order to attract 'clients', facilities and services offered have to be of a very high standard. Fitness clubs (e.g. Fitness First) are good examples of private-sector organisations.
- **Voluntary-sector organisations** are **owned and managed by members** on a voluntary basis and trade on a break-even basis. For example, many local tennis and rugby clubs are run by the members for the members, with any profit made being reinvested in the club, perhaps to improve facilities.

Compulsory competitive tendering

Compulsory competitive tendering involves local authorities inviting competitive bids or tenders from interested parties to run their sports and/or recreation services. The choice of organisation to run a particular service is based on the principle of **best value**. This means choosing the organisation that can give a high-quality service at the lowest possible cost, so that the public gets the most benefit. Prices may be higher than those offered when local authority subsidies are applied to certain groups of society, but higher quality facilities and staff training lead to an improved service.

Ways to increase participation

Ways in which local authorities can achieve Sport England's aim of increased participation include:

- creating links between schools, voluntary clubs and local authority facilities
- ensuring that their facilities and activities are fully promoted
- creating more opportunities for special interest target groups, such as the elderly, ethnic minorities, disabled people and the unemployed, at affordable prices
- developing the social side of facilities as well as the sporting aspects

What the examiners will expect you to be able to do

- An understanding of the key characteristics of mob football as an example of a popular recreational activity is important, both in isolation and in comparison to football as an organised rational activity.
- You should be able to demonstrate knowledge of the development and influence of public schools from their pre-Arnold era through to the post-Clarendon reforms.
- The all-consuming belief in the power of games to instil positive qualities in young gentlemen and society in general should be revised and understood.
- Late-nineteenth century and twentieth century developments in state PE should be understood in relation to their aims, content and teaching methods.
- While specific dates are not essential to gain marks, an awareness of the correct chronological order of educational reforms will earn marks.

Questions will be set asking for specific knowledge of initiatives in school PE and sport. You should be aware of:

- benefits of sports college status for pupils and the community in general
- key features of TOPS programmes

When more general questions are set in relation to mass participation and sports excellence, knowledge of relevant initiatives in school PE is required.

- You may be required to compare the features or aims of, for example, the public and private sectors as described above.
- You should know the meaning of compulsory competitive tendering ('best value') and at least two key features of providing the best quality service at the lowest possible cost.

Historical and social influences on modern-day sport

Mass participation

The idea behind mass participation in sport is that everyone should have the chance to take part as often as they would like. However, reality does not always match the principle of equal opportunities in 'Sport for All'. Target and special interest groups are sections of society identified by Sport England as needing special attention. The aim is to raise participation levels to try and ensure that these groups have equality of sporting opportunity. Examples of target groups include ethnic minorities, lower social-class groups, women and disabled people.

Initiatives to increase participation

Home country organisations

Sport England is a key organisation involved in raising participation levels among the general population. The aims of **more people** and **more places** are being implemented through a variety of schemes.

The more people initiative is being promoted by:

- Active Schools — TOPS/Activemark and Sportsmark are encouraging active participation in schools.
- Active Sports — this provides lottery funding for facilities and equipment for nine targeted sports, including athletics and basketball, to help school-age children achieve more from their chosen sport.
- Active Communities — this encourages increased participation in sport by all sections of the community.

More places are being provided by:

- more efficient management of facilities
- lottery funding, which enables the building of more facilities for sport and recreation

Special interest groups

Women's Sports Foundation (WSF)

The WSF has a commitment to improving and promoting opportunities for women in sport at all levels. The key functions of the WSF are:

- to campaign for change to combat inequality in sport (mass participation)
- to raise the profile of British sportswomen, for example through national awards ceremonies
- to advise other organisations on women's sporting issues

Disability Sport England

The functions of Disability Sport England include:

- working to improve awareness of, and the image of, disabled sport
- educating the general public about the capabilities of the disabled
- promoting the benefits of sport and recreation to the disabled
- encouraging disabled people to play an active role in the development of their sport

Factors limiting the implementation of initiatives

There are constraints that limit the chances of people participating in sport regularly. These constraints may be based on opportunity, provision or esteem.

Opportunity refers to factors that affect the chance to take part, including:

- the attitudes of friends
- not having enough money to pay for the sport
- lack of time because of family or work commitments

Provision refers to more tangible features that influence participation, such as:
- lack of specialist facilities or access to such facilities (e.g. disabled access to swimming pools)
- lack of specialist equipment (e.g. wheelchairs for basketball)
- lack of appropriate activities (i.e. those that appeal to particular target groups such as the elderly)

Esteem refers to the perceptions held by others of an individual or group. Factors connected with esteem that limit participation in sport include:
- lack of self-confidence, low self-expectation and fear of rejection
- bullying
- discrimination (i.e. unfairness; imbalance of power between groups)
- lack of positive role models and low media coverage

Tip It is important to link appropriate constraints to particular special interest groups. For example, lack of time is more likely to be an issue for young mothers (because of work and family commitments) than it would be for an elderly person.

Participation in sport and physical activity

In addition to identifying causes of under-representation in sport by various groups in society, it is important to be aware of possible solutions to these problems.

Effects of race and religion
Some ethnic and religious groups are under-represented. Causes of this and some possible solutions are given in the table below.

Cause	Solution
Racism and racist abuse	Anti-racism publicity; stricter punishment of racist abuse
Religious observances	Single-sex provision for ethnic-minority women
Fewer role models, particularly as coaches and managers	Training more ethnic minority sports coaches and administrators

Effects of gender
Women generally participate in sport less than men do. Causes of this and some possible solutions are given in the table below.

Cause	Solution
Less media coverage; fewer role models	Increase media coverage of women's sport; promote positive role models (e.g. Kelly Holmes)
Negative effects of schools' PE programmes	Provide more choice of activities and kit for schoolgirls
Lack of time; child-care responsibilities	Provide child care at leisure centres
Traditionally, lack of own disposable income	More social acceptance of women having jobs and financial independence

Women's own attitudes can act as barriers to participation. These include:

- lack of self-confidence — 'not good enough'
- lack of motivation — 'too tired' or 'no time'
- being put off by the myth of sport making women too 'masculine'
- poor self-image — some women feel they are too unhealthy or unfit to participate in sport

Effects of disability

Generally, the disabled have a low-level of participation in sport. Causes of this and some possible solutions are given in the table below.

Cause	Solution
Myths and stereotypes surrounding the disabled	Educate people about the disabled
Lower income levels	Increase investment in disabled sport to make it more affordable
Few role models	Increase media coverage of disabled sport
Poor access to facilities; poor access in and around them	Provide transport to facilities; improve access in and around them
Few competitions and clubs	More competitions at all levels; more clubs for the disabled in a wider variety of sports (e.g. by adapting or profiling* of sports)

* Separating disabled individuals into categories, so they are participating with others of a similar 'level' of disability

Effects of social class and wealth

Social class refers to income, background, societal status and education. Playing and watching sport costs money. The more money a person has, the greater the opportunities to take part in or to watch sports. There is also a free choice of participating in sport at public, private or voluntarily-run facilities.

In Britain, social class, wealth discrimination and the consequent inequality of opportunity are centuries old. In pre-industrial times, the upper and lower social classes pursued separate sports. For example, hunting was exclusively for the upper classes and mob football was for the lower classes. As a result of the industrial revolution, a new middle class was created that participated in sport 'for the love of the game' and played a key role in the formation of the national governing bodies and subsequent rule development. A three-tier society is still broadly in evidence in the UK today:

- upper class — polo, equestrianism and field sports
- middle class — hockey, tennis and rugby union
- lower or working class — darts, rugby league and snooker

There is also evidence that lower socioeconomic background leads to less participation in sport. This is due to factors such as cost, lower levels of health and fitness, low self-esteem and lack of opportunities to take up sport or to become role models in leadership positions. Subsidised provision that encourages participation in local community schemes can help to overcome these barriers. Such schemes also serve important functions as diversions from crime and general social disorder.

What the examiners will expect you to be able to do

Questions on mass participation in sport occur frequently. You may be asked to name initiatives of organisations such as Sport England that are designed to increase participation.

Another key requirement is to be able to relate factors limiting participation in sport to particular special-interest groups. It is a good idea to answer this type of question under the three headings 'opportunity', 'provision' and 'esteem', as this may help you to remember a range of different constraints that affect participation. There are four clearly defined target groups you need to revise — ethnic minorities, women, disabled people and lower social-class groups. These groups should be considered in terms of the causes of low levels of participation in sport together with possible solutions to these causes.

Questions
&
Answers

Τhis section of the guide contains questions that are similar in style to those you can expect to see in Unit Test 2. The questions cover the three areas of the specification identified in the Content Guidance section. Each question is followed by an average or poor response (Candidate A) and an A-grade response (Candidate B). You should try to answer these questions yourself, so that you can compare your answers with the candidates' responses. In this way, you should be able to identify your strengths and weaknesses in both subject knowledge and exam technique.

Examiner's comments

All candidate responses are followed by examiner's comments. These are preceded by the icon *e* and indicate where credit is due. In the weaker answers they point out areas for improvement, specific problems and common errors, such as vagueness, irrelevance and misinterpretation of the question.

Mock paper

This section concludes with of a mock Unit 2 test, accompanied with a mark scheme. Once you have completed your revision and worked through the sample questions on pages 37–47, you should try to complete this test under exam conditions. This means within the allowed time of 1 hour 15 minutes, in a silent environment, without reference to books or notes.

The **mark scheme** is provided so that you, or perhaps a teacher, can mark your responses. The potential difficulty here is deciding if a point is relevant when the exact wording of the mark scheme has not been used. You should also be aware that a particular point on the mark scheme may only be awarded once, even if a number of alternative answers are given. For example, 'fun/enjoyment/non-serious' in relation to a feature or characteristic of play could all come under the same marking point.

The front of your Unit 2 test paper will provide the following information:

Sport and physical education
Unit 2
Time allowed: 1 hour 15 minutes

Instructions
- **Answer *three* from four questions.**
- **Cross-through any 'rough work' that you do not want to be marked.**

Information
- **The maximum mark for this paper is 57.**
- **Mark allocations are shown in brackets.**

Quality of written communication
- **You will be assessed on your ability to use appropriate form and style of writing, to organise relevant information clearly, and to use specialist vocabulary, where appropriate.**

The nature and characteristics of physical activities

(a) PE teachers aim to develop their pupils' knowledge and values. Identify values and benefits to be gained from a positive school PE experience. (4 marks)

(b) Play is often considered to be an educational experience. What can children learn through play? (4 marks)

(c) What are the main characteristics of sport? (5 marks)

(d) Apart from games, identify all other areas of activity within the National Curriculum for PE. (3 marks)

(e) State how a winner is determined in each of the following categories of sport:
- athletic
- game
- gymnastic (3 marks)

(f) Competitive sport can be analysed using components such as 'structural', 'strategic' and 'technical'. Explain the terms *'structural'* and *'strategic'*. (2 marks)

Total: 21 marks

■ ■ ■

Candidates' answers to Question 1

Candidate A

(a) Having a positive PE experience may encourage you to take up sport when you are older ✓. This can improve your health and general wellbeing ✓. Having a good experience can also help encourage your children participate in sport.

> 🖉 The first two sentences earn marks as they are linked to the 'preparation for leisure' and 'improved health' values of PE. The final sentence is vague and confusing. The answer is too brief and lacks a range of different points. Candidate A scores 2 marks.

Candidate B

(a) A positive PE experience can lead to:
- the development of physical skills ✓
- health benefits ✓
- knowledge of the rules of a sport ✓
- help in getting a job or career in sport ✓
- an improvement in self-confidence ✓
- making friends and improving social skills ✓
- knowledge of tactics used in a sport

e The first six points are all worth a mark. The final point about tactics is too similar to the earlier point about rules to be credited. This answer is written in an examiner-friendly way with a brief introduction and the key points listed as bullets. More points have been made than there are marks available, to try to ensure full marks are earned. Candidate B scores all 4 marks.

Candidate A

(b) Children can learn how to play fairly and respect the rules of a game ✓. They can learn about sportsmanship and accepting defeat. They also learn basic skills, such as throwing and catching ✓.

e This is an example of an answer that is factually correct but focuses too much on one point — fair play. The second sentence repeats the first, so a mark cannot be awarded. Without the practical example, the 'basic skills' point may not have been awarded because 'skills' could relate to physical, mental or social development. Candidate A scores 2 marks.

Candidate B

(b) • Children can learn how to interact with others ✓.
  • They learn fundamental motor skills by playing with such things as balls ✓.
  • They learn cognitive skills by problem solving ✓.
  • They learn how to cooperate and work together as a team ✓.
  • When making up their own games, they learn creative skills ✓.
  • They learn how to play safely ✓.

e All six points are relevant and answer the question in a clear and succinct manner. Use of practical examples is further evidence of good exam practice, as is the fact that more points have been made than there are marks available. Candidate B scores all 4 marks.

Candidate A

(c) Sport is played professionally at high levels ✓. People such as Wayne Rooney earn lots of money from playing football for a living. He is my role model. I want to be like him because he plays at a high level for my favourite club. The skills he produces on the pitch are fantastic which again makes me want to be like him ✓.

e Although the use of practical examples to illustrate your understanding is to be encouraged, in this case too much focus on one person has limited the number of marks gained. Repeating the point about a professional playing for high rewards at a high level means only 1 mark can be gained because the characteristics are so similar. Reference to high skill levels gains a second mark. A variety of points should have been made in answer to this relatively simple question. Candidate A scores only 2 of the 5 available marks.

Candidate B

(c) Sport has a number of characteristics, such as:
- competitiveness and the will to win ✓
- rules ✓
- high fitness demands ✓
- governing bodies (e.g. the FA) ✓
- use of specialist equipment ✓
- officials that make decisions

e Just enough relevant points are made to gain maximum marks. The final point cannot be awarded a mark because it repeats the point about 'rules'. It would have been a good idea to make one or two more points, in case of vagueness or more repetition. Missing out on maximum marks on relatively easy questions can make a significant difference to the final grade achieved. Unless a specific number is asked for in the question, always make more points than there are marks available. Candidate B scores all 5 marks.

Candidate A

(d) In my PE lessons I play a lot of sport and different games such as football, cricket, and tennis. I also do lots of running.

e This answer is a vague attempt to earn a few marks despite a lack of knowledge of the areas of activity defined in National Curriculum PE. The candidate should have highlighted or underlined 'Apart from games' in the question before starting to answer. This would have ensured that games were not included in the answer. If the final point about running had been linked to athletics, then it would have earned a mark. Candidate A fails to score.

Candidate B

(d) National Curriculum PE has a number of different areas of activity:
- gymnastics and dance ✓
- swimming and athletics ✓
- outdoor and adventurous activities ✓

e This is an examiner-friendly way of giving an answer in a relevant, clear and succinct manner. All areas of activity identified are correct, for full marks.

Candidate A

(e) In athletics the winner is determined by time and distance. In games it is the greatest number of points ✓. In gymnastics you win if the judges give you the most points ✓.

e The first answer is too vague. Fastest time or furthest distance would have been correct for athletic activities. The games and gymnastics answers each earn 1 mark.

Candidate B

(e) The winner in athletic sports is decided by a quantitative measure (e.g. in high jump, it is the greatest height) ✓. Games rely on domination of territory (e.g. scoring more tries than the opposition in rugby) ✓. In gymnastic sports the winner is decided by points awarded for quality of movement (i.e. qualitative measurement) ✓.

℮ This is an excellent answer that clearly shows understanding of how a winner is decided in each category. In each case, there is an explanation and a practical example. Candidate B scores all 3 marks.

Candidate A

(f) A sport such as football has rules to play to and lots of decisions to be made.

℮ No marks can be awarded because the answer does not relate to 'structure' and 'strategy' as required and emphasised by the question.

Candidate B

(f) The structure of a sport is the rules and regulations ✓. The strategy of a sport is the tactics and decision-making ✓.

℮ This is a succinct answer containing relevant points. Candidate B scores both marks.

℮ **Overall, Candidate A scores 8 marks out of 21; Candidate B scores full marks.**

Question 2

Historical developments in sport and PE

(a) The development of different sports was greatly influenced by public schools in the late nineteenth century. State *three* changes made to sports by public schools. (3 marks)

(b) Explain the terms *'athleticism'* and *'muscular Christianity'*. (3 marks)

(c) During the late nineteenth century, modern sports replaced traditional mob games. What social and economic changes accounted for this development? (6 marks)

(d) The physical activities offered by state elementary schools changed during the first half of the twentieth century. Describe and explain these changes. (7 marks)

(e) Increasing participation in physical activity within a community is considered a positive act in today's 'egalitarian' society. How do the reasons for increasing participation differ between *local authority* clubs and *voluntary* clubs? (4 marks)

(f) National sports organisations, such as Sport England, have devised various schemes to introduce children into sport and develop their talents. Using examples, explain how such schemes help to achieve these aims. (5 marks)

(g) TOP Sport in England is an example of a primary school initiative. Describe TOP Sport. (4 marks)

Total: 32 marks

■ ■ ■

Candidates' answers to Question 2

Candidate A

(a) Public schools wanted to change sports for a number of reasons. They wanted sports to be less violent ✓ and become more civilised. The behaviour of players became more controlled, with less violence. This was because the mob games led to far too many injuries and damage to property.

e This answer focuses too much on material that, although factually correct, is irrelevant, such as the features of mob football. It is more of a 'why changes occurred' answer, rather than a *statement* of actual changes made. Candidate A scores only 1 mark.

Candidate B

(a) Three changes made to sport by public schools in the late nineteenth century were:
- the introduction of rules ✓
- that sport became more civilised and less violent ✓
- that equipment and specialist kit were provided ✓

e The question asks for a specific number of points. This answer shows how to set out a list of sufficiently varied and relevant answers to gain full marks.

Candidate A

(b) They were terms that mixed religion with sport. They involved teamwork, fair play and the idea that performance could be more important than winning.

> To earn marks, the answer needs to show understanding of *both* athleticism *and* muscular Christianity. This answer is mainly about features of muscular Christianity and 2 marks could have been gained if the link had been made. Candidate A fails to score.

(b) Athleticism involves physical values ✓ and striving to do your best ✓. Muscular Christianity was more about ethical values such as fair play ✓ and making you a better Christian ✓.

> Candidate B scores all 3 marks. There is clear evidence of understanding of both the terms. These are succinctly described and two points are made in each case, to help ensure that the maximum marks are gained.

Candidate A

(c) Mob games were replaced by more modern sports because of injuries to workers ✓. This meant production was lost. Damage to property was no longer accepted in modern society ✓. There was less space to play mob games in urban areas ✓. Transport developments encouraged the more modern games to develop.

> This is an excellent answer in terms of the economic changes that accounted for the development of modern sports, for 3 marks. However, no social changes are given. This is an example of an unbalanced answer that responds to only one part of a question.

Candidate B

(c) Social changes leading to the demise of mob games included:
- discouragement by the church because they conflicted with Christian morals ✓
- modern sports promoting more socially accepted characteristics, rather than violence ✓
- modern sports being used as a form of 'social control' ✓

Economic changes that led to mob games being replaced included:
- damage to property ✓
- less time being available because of industrialisation ✓
- the chance of injury to the work force ✓

> In response to the question set, this answer covers both social and economic factors that accounted for the development of modern sports. All six points are correct and relevant and the maximum 6 marks are therefore gained. If time allows at the end of an exam, it is good practice to try to add one or two more points to such answers. This is in case any of the answers given are irrelevant, repetitive or vague. You should use all the time available in an exam to try to impress the examiners and gain as many marks as possible.

Candidate A

(d) In the late nineteenth and early twentieth centuries there was a focus on drill (mainly military) ✓. As the twentieth century began, a more therapeutic approach to drill was introduced ✓. There was also recognition of different ages and sexes of children ✓. Following the Second World War, facilities were improved ✓ and a more child-centred approach was taken to teaching PE ✓.

   e One part of the question — a description of changes to state PE — has been very well answered and earns 4 marks. The final point would receive a mark, had the sub-maximum 4 marks not already been achieved. However, there is no *explanation* of these developments, as required by the question.

Candidate B

(d) Military drill was initially taught to boys only ✓ as preparation for their military service ✓ and also to improve health and fitness ✓. In the early twentieth century, a more therapeutic approach, based on the Swedish system of drill, was introduced ✓. This was due to more emphasis being placed on children having fun ✓. As the twentieth century progressed there was more use of apparatus in schools ✓ and teachers were able to use their own initiative to teach ✓.

   e This answer is made in a chronologically correct manner and includes relevant points that describe and explain developments in state PE in the early twentieth century. Candidate B scores all 7 marks.

Candidate A

(e) Private-sector clubs, such as David Lloyd fitness centres, provide top-level facilities but can cost a lot of money. Public-sector clubs, such as local authority leisure centres, are cheaper but facilities are not as good. Voluntary-sector clubs, such as my hockey club, aim to provide good facilities to get more members ✓.

   e This answer has a clear structure and is quite well written, but unfortunately *it does not answer the question set*. It is the start of an analysis of the differences between public, private and voluntary sectors, which focuses too much on facilities and does not relate to reasons for increasing participation. Candidate A scores only 1 mark.

Candidate B

(e) Local authorities want to increase participation to improve the health of individuals ✓ and, therefore, to create a healthier society ✓. There are often benefits to the community. Voluntary clubs want to attract more members ✓ so they have a better chance of winning competitions ✓.

   e This is a succinct, relevant answer. Both parts of the question are answered, producing a balanced response that earns the maximum 4 marks. With the relatively limited time available in the unit test, it is this type of concise answer that is needed to do well.

question

Candidate A

(f) Sport England has a lot of schemes for children, such as TOPS ✓, Active Schools and Active Communities. These schemes help develop children's abilities and improve their chances of sporting success and winning more medals.

> *e* This answer gives a number of relevant examples as required by the question, but the mark scheme may allow a sub-maximum of just 1 mark for these. The rest of the answer is far too brief for a 5-mark question and lacks relevant detail about *how* talent-development schemes help children take up, and progress in, sport. Candidate A scores only 1 mark.

Candidate B

(f) A variety of national organisations such as Sport England and the Youth Sports Trust ✓ have developed programmes to introduce children into sport. These include TOPS. TOPS provides equipment to use ✓ and training for coaches ✓ to help make sport fun for children. They adapt sports (e.g. tag rugby) ✓, with different rules and, perhaps, smaller balls ✓.

> *e* Candidate B gains all 5 available marks. The answer gives a relevant example and then *explains* this appropriately, as required by the question. An additional example or further explanation point could have been given to help ensure maximum marks. Unless the question asks for a specific number of points, it is good exam technique to make more points than there are marks available.

Candidate A

(g) TOP Sport is a series of initiatives for children aged from 18 months to 18 years. These range from TOP Tots to TOP Sportsability. They aim to develop skills and fitness through schooling. As the schemes increase, more analysis and coaching becomes involved.

> *e* The points made are irrelevant and vague. The question requires a description of TOP Sport, which is one of the TOPS programmes. This should be the focus of the answer. However, Candidate A focuses on describing the range of TOPS programmes available. To make sure that you answer the question set, it might help to highlight key words or phrases in the question before starting to write your answer. Candidate A does not score.

Candidate B

(g) TOP Sport is supported and developed by the Youth Sports Trust ✓. It is designed to support teachers in their delivery of National Curriculum PE ✓ to 7–11 year olds ✓. Training is provided for teachers to deliver TOP Sport ✓. Bags containing adapted sports-related equipment ✓ are given to teachers to help them deliver TOP Sport. Teaching cards with lesson ideas on them are also provided ✓.

e Candidate B has answered the question set and included many relevant points on TOP Sport. More correct points are made than the maximum mark available, which is good exam practice. Candidate B scores all 4 marks.

e **Overall, Candidate A scores 10 marks out of 32; Candidate B scores full marks.**

Historical and social influences on modern-day sport

(a) How might a person's ethnic background influence his/her participation in physical activity? (4 marks)

(b) Apart from 'adaptations', in what other ways can the participation of people with disabilities be increased? (3 marks)

(c) What social and economic barriers do women face today when attempting to participate in sport or physical activity? (4 marks)

Total: 11 marks

■ ■ ■

Candidates' answers to Question 3

Candidate A

(a) Ethnic background links to race. Race links to the colour of a person's skin. If you are from an ethnic minority group, you may take part less in sport because you may fear rejection by a sports club ✓ and have low self-esteem. This fear may be due to physical threats ✓ and abuse. Racial discrimination can lower participation levels.

e This answer illustrates how a candidate can focus too much on a particular point or two. Though these are explained very well, repeating the same point does not earn marks. To gain more marks, the answer needs to cover a range of different points. Candidate A scores 2 marks.

Candidate B

(a) People's ethnic background influences their involvement in physical activity, because racial discrimination may lower participation ✓. There may be fewer role models in certain sports ✓ but more in others to encourage participation. Higher values placed on education as opposed to sport may limit participation ✓. Lower levels of self-esteem may put off ethnic minorities from taking part in sport ✓.

e Four relevant and sufficiently varied points are made to earn full marks.

Candidate A

(b) Disabled people often struggle to get around leisure centres ✓. They need lifts and ramps to help improve this situation. If television gave more time to disabled sport, it might help increase participation as more role models might be created ✓.

e This answer addresses the question set and makes relevant points backed up with examples. All it lacks is a sufficient range of points to earn full marks. Candidate A scores 2 marks.

Candidate B

(b) Participation of disabled people in sport could be increased by providing special times for them at leisure centres ✓. More clubs could be set up for them to join ✓, with specialist coaching provided ✓. If more media coverage was given, for example of the paralympics, it might increase participation by the disabled ✓.

e Candidate B scores all 3 marks. This is an excellent answer, which contains four relevant points to try to ensure maximum marks are gained.

Candidate A

(c) Women still have to look after children more than men ✓. Many sports are seen as too strenuous for women to take part in ✓. Myths and stereotypes still exist about what women can do.

e This answer is a little too brief and focuses purely on 'social' factors. In answer to a 'what' question, bullet point lists of social and economic factors linked to women's lack of participation in physical activity would suffice. No specific number of points is asked for, so relevant educated guesses could be made to try and gain more marks. Candidate A scores 2 of the 4 available marks.

Candidate B

(c) • Sexual discrimination still exists in society today ✓.
• Many males see sport as their preserve ✓.
• Women tend to have jobs that pay them less ✓.
• Women have less media coverage and fewer role models to aspire to ✓ and less funding and sponsorship ✓.

e A range of social and economic barriers affecting women's participation in sport is given. Once again, more correct points are made than there are marks available and Candidate B scores full marks.

e **Overall, Candidate A scores 6 marks out of 11; Candidate B scores 11 marks.**

**mock
paper**

Unit 2

Answer *three* from four questions

(1) (a) The link between exercise and health has influenced the development of PE syllabuses.

    (i) What were the significant developments between the 1904 and 1919 syllabuses? (4 marks)

    (ii) What were the major factors that influenced these developments? (4 marks)

  (b) National Curriculum PE today requires schools to promote physical activity and a healthy lifestyle.

    (i) How could this be achieved within the modern-day curriculum? (3 marks)

    (ii) In a society that is relatively wealthy and has a well-developed National Health Service, why is it still necessary to promote physical activity for reasons of health? (3 marks)

    (iii) Aerobics is a popular activity among young women. Give reasons why this is the case. (4 marks)

Total: 18 marks

(2) At the beginning of the twentieth century, the extent and nature of people's participation in sport were influenced by their social class and gender.

  (a) Describe the differences in the sports played and the roles undertaken by the upper/middle classes and the working class. Illustrate your answer with appropriate examples. (5 marks)

  (b) Discuss the reasons why people from the working class had fewer opportunities to participate in sport than those from the upper and middle classes. (4 marks)

  (c) At the beginning of the twentieth century, why were women discouraged from taking part in a number of competitive sports? (3 marks)

  (d) Why is it that girls have a greater tendency to drop out of sport and physical activity than boys? (3 marks)

  (e) Why does the government promote sport within socially and economically deprived areas? (3 marks)

Total: 18 marks

(3) Historically, individuals have engaged in a variety of leisure and recreational activities. Modern-day opportunities are varied and come from a range of providers.

  (a) Local authorities are responsible for the provision of leisure facilities for members of their local community.

    (i) What *differing objectives* may a local authority 'leisure centre' have compared with a private-sector sports club (e.g. Fitness First)? (4 marks)

    (ii) The introduction of compulsory competitive tendering and 'best value' has altered the relationship between private and public provision of leisure. Why were these practices introduced and what effects did they have? (5 marks)

(iii) The high degree of public provision implies that the state considers leisure and recreation to be of significant value to the individual. Why should this be the case? (4 marks)

(b) One historical form of physical recreation was the playing of mob games — for example, the Ashbourne mob-football game. What was the attitude of the authorities towards such games and why was that attitude held? (5 marks)

Total: 18 marks

(4) During the nineteenth and early twentieth centuries, very clear distinctions were maintained between social classes in terms of their participation in sport and physical activity.

(a) Using appropriate examples, explain how such distinctions were maintained. (3 marks)

(b) Between 1860 and 1900, many national governing bodies for sport were established in England. Explain why these national governing bodies were formed. (3 marks)

(c) In the UK, a person's participation in sport and physical activity may be influenced by a variety of social factors. How might a person's ethnic background influence their participation in physical activity? (4 marks)

(d) Disability Sport England has a responsibility to promote participation in sport for people with all forms of disability.

(i) Physical disability is one major category; state two other categories of disability. (2 marks)

(ii) Some sports have been adapted to meet the requirements of people with particular disabilities. In order to retain the nature of sport, what factors need to be considered? (3 marks)

(iii) Apart from adaptations, in what other ways can the participation of people with disabilities be raised? (3 marks)

Total: 18 marks

Mark scheme

In the following mark scheme:

- each bullet point represents a single mark, which can only be awarded once
- a forward slash (/) indicates alternatives that can be credited for a particular point on the scheme
- 'equivalent' means allow any equivalent answers

Mark scheme for Question 1

(a) (i) *4 marks for four of the following points:*
- more therapeutic approach/health/fitness/strenuous/active
- fewer free-standing exercises/reduction in formal nature of lessons/use of equipment
- division in work between older and younger children
- more opportunities for free movement for (younger) children
- some introduction of games for younger children/teamwork/interaction
- older children still had exercise/unison work

(a) (ii) *4 marks for four of the following points:*
- control moved to the medical department of the Board of Education/away from military preparation
- reflected social concerns over the health of the working class
- continuing perception that older children still needed discipline
- desire for creation of an obedient work force/military
- an understanding of the value of play and fun for children
- First World War convalescence showed the value of exercise/games
- physical training became a compulsory part of teacher training
- increasing influence of women PE teachers

(b) (i) *3 marks for three of the following points:*
- use of a (range) of health-related fitness activities/range of activities
- opportunities to develop individual programme/choose activities that are more likely to be pursued in later life
- provide information on effects of lack of exercise/poor diet
- arrange taster sessions at local health/sports/fitness centres/clubs/ encourage extra-curricular activity
- National Curriculum for PE compulsory at all key stages, so physical activity experienced by all pupils aged 5-16

(b) (ii) *3 marks for three of the following points:*
- research indicates that children are less active/lack of local opportunity
- not walking to school/playing in the street/fears over safety
- other recreational opportunities/computers/television/or equivalent
- general lack of public knowledge about the health effects of lack of exercise
- supports physical growth
- preventing ill health/off-setting health risks

(b) (iii) *4 marks for four of the following points:*
- reflects society pressure to attain the 'ideal shape'/desired body shape
- seen to be acceptable/society sees it as being female-appropriate/promoted to women
- health/fitness attainment has become fashionable/seen to be important
- use of music/fashionable clothing makes it more popular
- has fewer of the drawbacks of outdoor sport/non-competitive/non-contact/female environment
- as an individual activity it can be done at a convenient time/fitted around work/family or equivalent
- enjoyable/fun/cheap/social/recreational/improves health

Mark scheme for Question 2

(a) *5 marks for five of the following points (maximum 4 marks per section):*
Upper/middle classes:
- amateur sports
- sports requiring facilities/resources/equipment (or reverse — working class did not have them)
- undertook leadership role/captain
- examples — rowing/rugby union/tennis/cricket/field sports
- control of sport/NGBs/agents/sponsors/patrons/heads of sport

Working class:
- sports offering professionalism
- examples — soccer/boxing/jockey (horse racing)/rugby league
- undertook subservient/subordinate role
- ground staff/maintain equipment/carry equipment
- spectating role

(Note that you do not get credit for 'mob football'.)

(b) *4 marks for four of the following points:*
- lack of leisure/free time
- lack of money/resources/poor diet/poor health/few facilities
- restrictive membership schemes/regulations
- amateur regulations
- limited demand for professionals in sport
- traditional working-class sports (such as fighting contests between animals) were frowned upon by middle class/considered uncivilised/banned/made illegal
- limited space in urban areas for traditional sports (such as mob games)
- encouraged to become spectators

(c) *3 marks for three of the following points:*
- sexual discrimination by men/outcasts/unwelcome
- based on gender stereotyping/must not compete with male role/not ladylike/very masculine/rough/aggressive

- women considered to be the weaker sex/deemed unable to take part in strenuous, physical activity
- believed that strenuous activity might interfere with women's fertility
- women required to take care of children/home
- women thought not to possess the need/drive/motivation to take part in sport (psychological)

(d) *3 marks for three of the following points:*
- lack of role models
- society's perception that sport is not for females/stereotyping/sport is for boys
- not encouraged by peers/parents/family
- fewer clubs/teams/facilities/opportunities available
- girls' perception of sport/physical activity fails to meet aspirations of girls women/seen as being masculine/unattractive to boys
- lack/nature of media coverage/images

(e) *3 marks for three of the following points:*
- raise community spirit/develop sense of community/pride/togetherness/social friendships
- offset crime/anti-social behaviour
- provide aspirations/jobs/acquire new life skills/more employable
- improve infrastructure/improve facilities/encourage regeneration/national strategy
- for neighbourhood renewal/social inclusion/increase equal opportunity
- to increase participation/health
- to widen the base of talent identification/talent spotting
- to increase government popularity/political popularity

Mark scheme for Question 3

(a) (i) *4 marks for four of the following points (maximum 3 marks per section):*
Local government:
- obliged to provide a service for local community/the public
- provide opportunities for disadvantaged groups in the local community
- provide opportunities for all through a greater range of activities
- provide value for money from rates/council tax
- only cover running costs

Private:
- make a surplus/profit
- aim services at a socially narrower range of customers
- offer a degree of exclusivity/restricted membership
- have no community service ethic/but may do so to enhance company image
- wider range of exclusive facilities/equipment/services, e.g. personal trainers/coaches

(ii) *5 marks for five of the following points (maximum 3 marks per section):*

Why?

- local authority facilities were often seen to be poorly managed because of lack of accountability
- provided poor value for money to local taxpayer/decline in provision
- lived in a subsidy culture
- reduction in central government funding for local government/particular effect on leisure and recreation

Effects:

- required local authority staff to bid for the right to manage facilities/against competition from private firms
- required commitments on standard of provision and amount of provision/public consultation
- improved quality of provision/monitoring of quality
- while maintaining community provision for disadvantaged

(a) (iii) *4 marks for four of the following points:*
- leisure enhances fitness/health/relieves stress
- by providing socialisation experiences/transferable skills
- by allowing the individual to exercise/creative involvement/for recreation/relaxation
- enhances work activity/productivity
- provides opportunities for play/fun/enjoyment
- leisure and recreation should therefore be provided for all/as a right
- keeps young people involved in purposeful leisure/off the streets

(b) *5 marks for five of the following points (maximum 2 marks per section):*

Attitude:
- authorities disliked mob games
- wished to ban/restrict them

Why?
- games were violent and disorderly/vulgar
- lack of rules/controlling authority
- threat to life and limb/dangerous
- threat to property/land
- disruption of production during and after the game
- fears that such large gatherings would bring possibility of insurrection
- (Church) disliked the gambling/drunkenness/lewd behaviour
- desire of the middle classes to direct the masses to more worthwhile pursuits

Mark scheme for Question 4

(a) *3 marks for three of the following points:*
- membership rules of clubs devised to exclude working class/exclusive to 'old boys'

**mock
paper**

- use of amateur regulations for competitions in order to prevent 'profession; from competing
- role specialisation within sport/lower classes performed supporting or speci; roles with the sport
- restricted access to facilities/club house/workday matches
- distinction made between 'gentlemen' and 'players'/professionals and amateu high class gentlemen/working classes and professionals (need both)
- examples from cricket/golf/rowing/tennis/rugby union (for middle/upper classes)
- membership fees kept high to exclude working class/insufficient leisure time/ money/resources/facilities
- encouraged to spectate (i.e. working classes)

(b) *3 marks for three of the following points:*
- diverse versions of games from public schools
- increased number of clubs/fixtures required more uniform rules to be established/administered/administrative
- greater mobility/more widespread competition/due to improvements in transport/also required codified rules
- rise in competition/need to oversee developed/devised/set up competitions/ tournaments
- greater need to vet competitors/teams/clubs in an attempt to maintain amateur code
- desire by middle/upper class to control sport/administer

(c) *4 marks for four of the following points:*
- ethnic stereotyping may discourage people away from some sports and encourage others (reference to 'stacking', i.e. individuals from particular ethnic groups being placed into certain positions in a sports team, for instance positions requiring speed, e.g. on the wing, as opposed to those requiring decision-making, e.g. central midfield)
- some ethnic groups are dominant in areas that lack sports facilities
- some values/practices associated with sports may conflict with religious observance
- racial discrimination/abuse/threats/may deter participation
- development of sporting ability not seen to be as important as development of other aspects of life, such as education, career/work, family/religious duties
- few role models in some sports/role models only exist in a limited number of sports
- perception/belief of cultural aspects/traditions/peer pressure/low self-esteem/ inferiority/fear of being rejected/not accepted
- ethnic minorities set up their own/different league/clubs

(d) (i) *2 marks for two of the following points:*
- sensory impairment/blind/deaf
- mental/learning difficulties

cerebral palsy
- transplant patients

(ii) *3 marks for three of the following points:*
- adaptations are based on the physical abilities of people to engage in physical activity/ability to move/execute skills
- which result in the modification of equipment
- modification of rules
- modification of environment
- consideration of safety
- to suit the disability, but retain the distinctive nature of the sport/maintain/challenge/competitiveness

(d) (iii) *3 marks for three of the following points:*
- improving physical access to/within sports facilities/special times/sessions for disability (e.g. lifts/ramps/wider doorways)
- setting up clubs/teams/competitions
- training of coaches/provision of specialist coaching
- use of campaigns/promotion/paralympians/special Olympians to inspire/role models/media
- increased awareness of needs/abilities in specialised training/courses/PE programmes/educating staff

Quality of written communication

The GCSE and GCE A/AS Code of Practice requires the assessment of the quality of written communication wherever candidates are required to write in continuous prose. In this unit, this assessment takes place for the script as a whole. The marking criteria are as follows:

- The candidate expresses moderately complex ideas clearly and reasonably fluently, through well-linked sentences and paragraphs. Arguments are generally relevant and well structured. There may be occasional errors of grammar, punctuation and spelling. (3 marks)
- The candidate expresses straightforward ideas clearly, if not always fluently. Sentences and paragraphs may not always be well connected. Arguments may sometimes stray from the point or be weakly presented. There may be some errors of grammar, punctuation and spelling, but not such as to suggest a weakness in these areas. (1–2 marks)
- Ideas are expressed poorly and sentences and paragraphs are not connected. There are errors of grammar, punctuation and spelling, showing a weakness in these areas. (0 marks)